Eleanor Roosevelt

by Ann Tatlock

FIRST LADIES Second to None

PURPLE TOAD
PUBLISHING

FIRST LADIES SECOND TO NONE

Abigail Adams
Dolley Madison
Edith Wilson
Eleanor Roosevelt
Hillary Rodham Clinton
Mary Todd Lincoln

PUBLISHER'S NOTE: The data in this book has been researched in depth, and to the best of our knowledge is factual. Although every measure is taken to give an accurate account, Purple Toad Publishing makes no warranty of the accuracy of the information and is not liable for damages caused by inaccuracies.

The stories at the beginning of chapters one and three contain fictional conversation based on what historical documents suggest might have been said.

Printing   2   3   4   5   6   7   8   9

Publisher's Cataloging-in-Publication Data
Tatlock, Ann.
   Eleanor Roosevelt / written by Ann Tatlock.
      p. cm.
            Includes bibliographic references and index.
            ISBN 9781624691768
1. Roosevelt, Eleanor, 1884-1962—Juvenile literature. 2. Roosevelt, Franklin D. (Franklin Delano), 1882-1945—Juvenile literature. 3. Presidents' spouses—United States—Biography—Juvenile literature. I. Series: First Ladies : Second to None.
   E807.1.R48 2016
   973.917092
         Library of Congress Control Number: 2015941827
eBook ISBN: 9781624691775

Contents

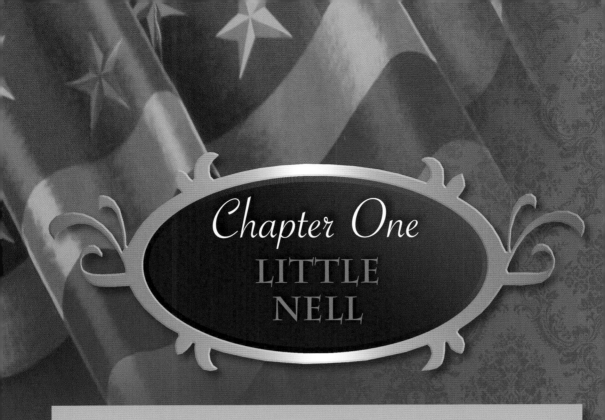

Chapter One
LITTLE NELL

'Come on, Nell! Let go! I'll catch you!" her father cried from far below.

Nell wailed again and clung to the sailor's sleeves. The icy Atlantic surged beneath her, tossing the tiny lifeboat under her parents and aunt. If she didn't fall just right, she'd miss the boat and sink to the bottom of the sea. The drop was too far!

The sailor who dangled the two-year-old over the ship's railing gripped her tightly again. "Hold on, Little Nell. Let go when I tell you." Nell screamed and thrashed as the sailor pried her fingers loose. "NOW!" he yelled. She felt his strong hands let go.

Little Nell and her parents had been sailing for Europe on the oceanliner SS *Britannic*. In thick fog, they were struck by another steamship, the SS *Celtic*. Pandemonium followed as the crew lowered lifeboats into the sea and passengers rushed to escape the damaged ships.

Miraculously, despite gaping holes in their hulls, neither ship was sinking. The people in the lifeboats returned to the ships—Nell and her family ended up on the *Celtic*—and the ships limped back to New York together. Only six people died in the disaster. Most of the crew and more than 1,300 passengers survived.

A severely damaged SS *Britannic* manages to stay afloat and make its way back to port in New York Harbor.

The *SS Celtic* while docked in Liverpool, England. The *Celtic*, after colliding with the *Britannic*, safely carried Eleanor and her family back to New York Harbor, in spite of its own damaged hull.

But the disaster took a different toll on Nell Roosevelt. For years afterward, she had nightmares of plunging into a storm-tossed sea. She was deathly afraid of water—and of many other things. She was afraid of the dark, of mice and snakes and other children. She was also afraid of not being liked by others. Looking back as an adult, she would describe her childhood as one long battle against fear.

There was another side to Little Nell, though. When she was six years old, she was traveling through Europe with her family. In Italy, her father hired a boy named Pietro to walk alongside her as she rode a donkey up into the mountains surrounding Sorrento. Every day, Pietro accompanied Nell as she rode.

One day Nell's father watched the pair return from their outing. He noticed that Pietro was riding the donkey and Nell was walking alongside! He ran out to confront the boy, but Nell told him it was her idea. She had insisted Pietro ride because he had cut his bare foot on a stone. Then she insisted that her father buy Pietro a pair of shoes, which he did. Pietro told

Eleanor and her father, Elliott Roosevelt

Nell that she was the kindest person he had ever met, because no one had ever noticed before that the rocks sometimes cut his feet.

Compassion and fear, fear and compassion—both claimed a stronghold in the heart of Little Nell. But Nell, who grew up to become First Lady Eleanor Roosevelt, learned to overcome her fears in order to devote her life to helping others. As she is often quoted as saying, "You gain strength, courage, and confidence by every experience in which you really stop to look fear in the face. . . . You must do the thing you think you cannot do."

Eleanor Roosevelt was born in 1884 to a family of wealth and prominence, but that didn't safeguard her from an unhappy childhood. Eleanor understood at a very young age that her mother was disappointed in her. Within the high-society circles of New York, mother Anna Roosevelt was renowned for her beauty and grace. Social standing was important to Anna, as was outward appearance. She considered her daughter homely and awkward and far too serious in nature. She nicknamed the child "Granny."

The mother's cruel name was in stark contrast to Elliott Roosevelt's nickname for his daughter. He affectionately called her Little Nell

Anna Roosevelt

Eleanor Roosevelt (right), her father, Elliott, and her brothers Gracie Hall and Elliott Jr. in New York. The special bond between father and daughter is evident in this photo.

after the gentle character in Charles Dickens' book *The Old Curiosity Shop.* There was a special bond between father and daughter. In his presence, Eleanor felt no judgment, only love and security.

Eventually, two sons, Elliott Jr. and Hall, joined the family. Knowing her mother favored the boys, Eleanor tried very hard to please her. When Anna suffered from migraine headaches, Eleanor spent hours rubbing her mother's temples to try to ease the pain. If Eleanor couldn't feel loved by her mother, at least she could feel useful.

Being of use to others was very important to young Eleanor, and in fact it was a trait instilled in her by her family. Her father, grandfather, aunts, and uncles all afforded her opportunities to work among the poor. Even as young as five or six years old, she was taken to poorhouses to serve hot meals, to hospitals to visit sick children, to the slums of New York to decorate Christmas trees.

Her uncle Theodore Roosevelt declared that the Roosevelts, who had so much, ought to fight for those less fortunate and to make a lasting change in people's lives. Later, Eleanor would write, "Very early I became conscious of the fact that there were people around me who suffered in one way or another."[1]

Theodore Roosevelt

Despite material wealth, Eleanor knew great suffering firsthand. Her beloved father, who was an alcoholic and was often violent, no longer lived at home. His brother, Theodore, had convinced him to move away from his family to try to be cured. In 1892, when Nell was only eight years old, her mother became sick with diphtheria and died.

Eleanor, Grandmother Hall, Aunt Tissie Mortimer, and Anna

Instead of living with their father, Eleanor and the boys were sent to live with their maternal grandmother, Mary Hall. One year later, Elliott Jr. succumbed to scarlet fever at age three.

Eleanor's father had never been able to stop drinking. In 1894, he jumped from his bedroom window. He lapsed into a coma and died. When her aunts told her the news, Eleanor cried herself to sleep.

Eleanor spent seven unhappy years in her grandmother's somber home. Just before her fifteenth birthday, though, she was sent to finishing school in

Her three years at Allenswood School in England were a happy time for Eleanor as she discovered the joy of making lasting friendships.

England. Allenswood was to be a turning point for the young lady. There, she became the favorite of the headmistress, and she was well-liked and popular among the other girls. For the first time, Eleanor began to know what it was like to feel happy and confident.

After three years at Allenswood, Eleanor was called home by her grandmother to make her social debut in New York. Eleanor was sorry to leave England and dreaded what she considered the ordeal of coming out as a debutant. But, dutifully, she obeyed her grandmother and returned to the United States.

Family Roots

The Roosevelt family traces its roots back to a Dutch settler named Claes Martenszen van Rosenvelt. He traveled from The Netherlands to New Amsterdam (later New York) in the steerage of a sailing ship in 1644. A common peasant, he eked out a living by farming on land that would later become part of Midtown Manhattan. Claes's son Nicolas was the first to spell the name as Roosevelt.

Claes's descendants proved to be shrewd businessmen who built their fortunes on banking, real estate, window glass, and West Indian sugar. Nicolas Roosevelt's son Johannes started the Oyster Bay branch of the family, while his other son, Jacobus, started the Hyde Park branch of the family. By the nineteenth century, the Roosevelts were among New York's oldest and most prominent and influential families.[2]

Nicolas Roosevelt was the first in the family to hold political office, as an alderman. Theodore Roosevelt, an Oyster Bay Roosevelt and a Republican, became the 26th President of the United States. Franklin Roosevelt, a Hyde Park Roosevelt and a Democrat, became the 32nd President of the United States.

Eleanor Roosevelt, like Theodore, was of the Oyster Bay branch. The man she eventually married, Franklin Roosevelt, was her fifth cousin once removed. When the two young Roosevelts married, Theodore said to Franklin, "Well, Franklin, there's nothing like keeping the name in the family."[3]

Theodore's family in 1903

Chapter Two

DANCING TO A DIFFERENT DRUMMER

Uncomfortable in her fancy Parisian gown, eighteen-year-old Eleanor surveyed the other debutants at the Waldorf-Astoria Hotel in New York. For months she had been dreading the lavish Assembly Ball, where she and other society girls would be introduced to and dance with eligible young men. She nervously adjusted one of the wire pins that held her hair in a loose pompadour. She had never felt at ease at fancy parties, and this one was no exception.

As she entered the ballroom with the other elegantly attired young women, she knew she was being compared unfavorably to them and to the memory of her mother, who had been one of the most beautiful debutants of all. Eleanor thought no one could possibly find her attractive. At 5 feet 11 inches, she was taller than the few gentlemen who asked her to dance.

She tried to be sociable, but for Eleanor the whole evening was "utter agony." Ashamed that she was the first woman in her mother's family not to be considered a belle, she made her excuses to the others and left the party early.[1]

Eleanor at age 15, about the time she enrolled at Allenswood School. A voracious reader with a quick mind, she excelled scholastically at Allenswood.

It is true that Eleanor was different from the other debutants, but the differences went far deeper than in simply how she looked. Eleanor had no genuine interest in feeling beautiful and popular. What she really wanted was to feel useful. She later confessed, "I have learned that true happiness lies in doing something useful with your life."

Like other wealthy society women of her time, Eleanor enrolled in the Junior League. The purpose of the League was to work among the poor living in New York's tenement houses. While many of the young women simply hosted fund-raising parties for the League, Eleanor chose to venture into the slums and work directly with those who lived in poverty. She taught calisthenics and dance to immigrant children at the Rivington Street Settlement House.[2] Dancing with the impoverished girls was far more appealing to Eleanor than dancing at any fancy ball.

Eleanor also became a member of the National Consumers League, a group dedicated to improving working conditions for women. She visited factories, sweatshops, and department stores where women worked long hours for little money. She wanted to help make their lives a little easier. Eleanor found the work so satisfying that she sometimes declined invitations to parties so that she could do volunteer work instead.

Although she may not have been looking to marry, a potential husband came looking for her.

Franklin Delano Roosevelt was a young Harvard University student whose path had seldom

Franklin Delano Roosevelt at Harvard

crossed that of his distant cousin, Eleanor. They had seen each other a few times at parties and family gatherings, but they didn't know each other well.

Recently their mutual uncle, Theodore Roosevelt, had become President of the United States. Only a few weeks after the Assembly Ball, both Franklin and Eleanor were invited to the White House for a New Year's reception and dinner. While there, they became reacquainted, and a month later Eleanor attended Franklin's twenty-first birthday party at his home at Hyde Park.

Eleanor and Franklin at Hyde Park

After that, they saw each other often. Franklin found Eleanor intelligent and thoughtful. She was able to hold a meaningful conversation, and that appealed to him. It didn't take Franklin long to decide that this was the woman he wanted by his side, the one who could help him achieve his goals.

Eleanor took longer to persuade. She couldn't believe this handsome and charming young man might be interested in anything more than a casual acquaintance with her. Even when he managed to slip away with her for a walk at Hyde Park to propose to her in private, she hesitated, unsure of what she had to offer him.

Franklin, patient but determined, persuaded her that he loved and needed her. Only then did she say yes.

They were married on March 17, 1905, in New York City. Her father's brother, President Theodore Roosevelt—or Uncle Teddy—escorted her down the aisle. After the wedding, the couple made their home at Franklin's Hyde Park estate overlooking the Hudson River.

Franklin and Eleanor Roosevelt with Anna and baby James

Eleanor settled into the life of a wife and mother. Much later she would write, "I had high standards of what a wife and mother should be and not the faintest notion of what it meant to be either a wife or a mother."[3] She would have to learn. Over the next ten years, she bore six children. The first was a girl named Anna, born in 1906. Five boys followed; the final one, John, was born in 1916. Sadly, their third child, Franklin Jr., died before he turned one year old.

Meanwhile, her husband graduated from both Harvard University and Columbia Law School. He began his career as an attorney on Wall Street in New York City. But it was politics that really drew him. In 1910 Franklin was nominated to run for the New York State Senate on the Democratic ticket, and he eagerly accepted. While he jumped headfirst into an active campaign, Eleanor, who was expecting another baby, stayed home to take care of their two children.

She supported her husband in his run for state senate, and was willing to move to the capital city of Albany should he win. But other than that she couldn't imagine how his election to political office might have anything to do with her. "I listened to all his plans with great interest," she said. But "it never occurred to me that I had any part to play."[4]

Shy and self-doubting, Eleanor would one day play a very large part in American politics.

Eleanor and Sara

Eleanor had a difficult relationship with Franklin's mother, Sara. She loved and respected Sara, but found her to be a hovering and overbearing mother-in-law.

Franklin was Sara Roosevelt's only child, and even when he was grown and married she seemed unable to let him go. She went so far as to build adjoining townhouses in New York City, with doors connecting her home with the young couple's home—doors through which, to Eleanor's dismay, Sara might appear at any time.

Sara lectured Eleanor on what Franklin should eat, how the children should be raised, what Eleanor should wear. She hired all of Eleanor's servants and chose all the furniture for her home. Eleanor even gave up her volunteer work because Sara considered it improper.

Eleanor said that in the first years of her marriage, "I was growing dependent on my mother-in-law, requiring her help on almost every subject, and never thought of asking for anything that I thought would not meet with her approval."[5]

Sara's domineering spirit drove Eleanor to tears. She knew this wasn't how she wanted to live. As Franklin became involved in politics and the family moved first to Albany and then to Washington, D.C., Eleanor turned her struggle with Sara into an opportunity to grow toward independence. She learned to make her own decisions. She began again to do work she enjoyed. She was finally able to say, "I was thinking things out for myself and becoming an individual."[6]

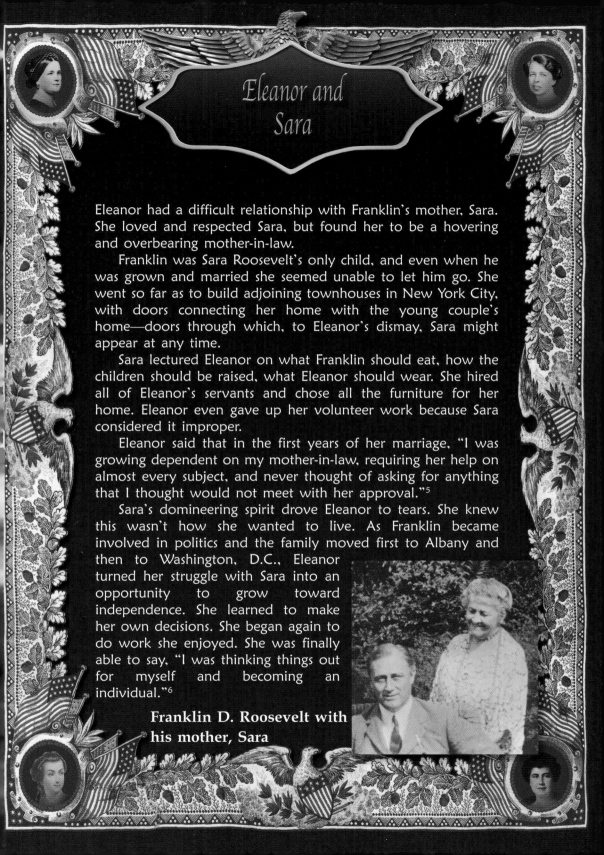

Franklin D. Roosevelt with his mother, Sara

Chapter Three
FINDING HER PLACE IN POLITICS

A warm breeze drifted in through the open window, beckoning the family to come out and enjoy the pleasures of Campobello Island. Every year, the family had vacationed there, at Sara Roosevelt's summer home off the coast of Maine. But the summer of 1921 was different, and Eleanor wasn't thinking about having fun. She was worried about her husband, who had just been diagnosed with polio. His legs were paralyzed, and she feared he would never walk again.

Sara Roosevelt wanted Franklin to retire from politics and settle into a life of leisure at Hyde Park. But Eleanor knew Franklin wanted to go back to work, and she supported his decision. She had brought in Dr. George Draper, a renowned polio specialist, to settle the issue.

Sara, of course, spoke first. "Dr. Draper," she said firmly, "I'm sure you will agree with me that Franklin is an invalid. He should therefore be retired to a wheelchair."

Eleanor disagreed. "This would be the worst thing you could do to him. He is not an invalid. If he fights, he may overcome his handicap."

"I ought to know what is best for my son," snapped Sara.

A rare photograph of Franklin Roosevelt in his wheelchair shows him visiting with a little girl while holding his dog Fala in his lap at Hyde Park, New York, in 1941.

Eleanor turned to the doctor. "We must do what you think best, Dr. Draper."

Eleanor's heart beat nervously as she waited for the doctor to respond. Finally he said, "Eleanor, you are right. He is not an invalid and there's no reason why he should be treated as one."[1]

It was a moment of triumph for Eleanor in more ways than she could know. Her strength and courage in making this decision helped change the course of history.

Franklin Roosevelt had already proved himself a capable politician and public figure in the years between 1910 and 1920. First he served two terms in the New York State Senate and afterward was appointed under the Woodrow Wilson administration as assistant secretary of the U.S. Navy.

Assistant Secretary of the Navy Franklin Roosevelt visits with the crew members of the USS _Texas_ during World War I.

These positions opened some unique opportunities for Eleanor and led to her early involvement in politics. As the wife of a state senator, Eleanor was constantly surrounded by politicians, and she found them and their ideas fascinating. She began to attend legislative sessions, where she learned the inner workings of the government.

In April 1917, while Franklin was assistant secretary of the navy, the United States entered World War I. As a Cabinet spouse, Eleanor returned to her first love: volunteer work. She became active with the Navy Relief Society and the American Red

Eleanor was happiest when her work made her feel useful to others.

Cross. Once again, although she was involved in traditional fund-raising, she preferred the hands-on work. At Union Station in Washington, D.C., she and other volunteers handed out sandwiches and coffee to thousands of servicemen as they were leaving for war. She also visited wounded sailors at St. Elizabeth's Hospital and successfully lobbied the government to improve the facility's services.

Two years after the war ended, the Democratic presidential candidate, James Cox, asked Franklin to run as his vice president. As Eleanor accompanied her husband on the campaign trail, she quietly soaked up volumes about American government and politics. In 1920, the first year women were allowed to vote, Eleanor voted for Cox and her husband. Though Cox didn't win the election, the name Roosevelt became nationally known. Franklin was well on his way to a successful career as a politician.

Then polio struck. Franklin would spend the next several years recovering, and that's when Eleanor really got busy. Franklin's friend and political adviser, Louis Howe, wanted to keep the Roosevelt name in the public eye and ear, so he asked Eleanor to step in and become even more active in the Democratic Party.

The couple in 1920 when Franklin was running for vice president on the Democratic ticket

She did. In the years ahead, she joined such agencies as The National League of Women Voters, the Women's Trade Union League, and the Women's Division of the New York State Democratic Committee. She worked as editor of *Women's Democratic News* and wrote dozens of magazine articles and newspaper editorials. She volunteered many hours at the Democratic Committee's headquarters, handed out campaign literature, spoke at hundreds of venues, and personally drove voters to and from the polls.

In addition, in 1926, Eleanor and two of her friends purchased the

Eleanor (second from left) and principal Marion Dickerman (fourth from left) pose with students in front of the Todhunter School for Girls in New York City.

Todhunter School for Girls on the East Side of New York City. Eleanor taught classes in history, government, and literature. She loved spending time with the students and would remain with the school until 1933.

Eleanor's primary concern in all this was improving the lives of working-class Americans, especially women and children. She worked to bring about child labor regulation and protective measures for women, including fair wages, affordable housing, and proper health care.

The day came when Franklin was ready to reenter politics. In 1928 he was elected governor of New York. The family moved again to Albany and Eleanor became First Lady of New York State. Reluctantly, she resigned from her political posts in the Democratic Party in order to take on the traditional role of a governor's wife.

But a new political partnership was about to form between husband and wife. Because of his paralysis, Franklin wasn't able to move about easily. Eleanor began to travel around the state for him, becoming his eyes

and ears. She inspected hospitals, schools, prisons, orphanages, and other state-supported institutions, going so far as to look into cooking pots on the stove and to check out the plumbing for herself. Afterward, she reported to Franklin on all that she had seen, and she made recommendations on how state government might better meet the needs of the people.[2]

Theirs was an effective and successful partnership, and Franklin was easily reelected for a second term as governor in 1930. By 1932, though, Franklin Roosevelt and Louis Howe had their sights set on the presidency. When Franklin ran on the Democratic ticket, he won by a landslide.

Eleanor Roosevelt was headed for the White House.

After being crippled by polio in 1921, Franklin walked with the aid of full-leg steel braces and crutches.

Louis Howe, Friend and Coach

At first, Eleanor was not impressed by Louis Howe. He was a small man who chain-smoked cigarettes while following her husband around like a shadow. He seemed to Eleanor an annoying little gnome.

In fact, Howe was one of Franklin Roosevelt's most trusted friends and advisers. During Franklin's 1920 campaign as the Democratic vice presidential nominee, Howe insisted that Eleanor accompany Franklin on the campaign trail.

Howe recognized there was not just one but two political figures in the Roosevelt marriage. During the long train rides between campaign stops, he made a point of talking with Eleanor. He discussed each day's events with her and asked her opinion of Franklin's speeches. Slowly, he won her friendship and admiration.

Howe encouraged Eleanor to join the women's division of the New York State Democratic Committee. She quickly rose to a leadership position where she was frequently invited to speak at meetings and other public gatherings. But speaking in front of people terrified her. In casual settings her voice was warm and friendly, but when she was nervous her voice became shrill, and she tended to giggle.

Howe stepped in to help. When Eleanor spoke publicly, he sat in the back of the hall and took notes. He went over her speeches with her, helping her to emphasize her strengths and minimize her giggles. "Have something to say," he coached, "say it, and then sit down."

Eleanor took his advice to heart. With Howe's help, Eleanor became a confident public speaker.

Louis Howe with Franklin Roosevelt

Chapter Four
A FIRST FOR FIRST LADIES

In May 1933, Franklin Roosevelt had just begun his first term as President of the United States. First Lady Eleanor Roosevelt, accompanied by Louis Howe, was driving to a very important meeting—though her attendance had not been announced.

Just outside Washington, D.C., a large gathering of jobless World War I veterans was camping. Many had been without work since the beginning of the Great Depression in 1929. They needed money for their families, and were hoping to persuade the government to give them the bonus money promised to them for having served in the war.

The previous summer, an even larger group of veterans and their families had gone to Washington to demand the bonus. These "Bonus Marchers" were not exactly welcomed by President Herbert Hoover. In fact, Hoover called on the army to clear the veterans' campsite. The Bonus Marchers were driven out and their belongings burned.

Now, a small group of them had returned, hoping the new president would give them what they wanted. Were they ever surprised to see First Lady Eleanor Roosevelt arrive at their camp!

Bonus Marchers camp out on the grounds of the Capitol Building in Washington, D.C., 1932. War veterans left jobless by the Great Depression, they hoped the government would respond to their plight.

Eleanor inspected the camp and drank coffee with the men. She listened to their grievances and told them what the President had in mind for them. While he was not able to give the men their bonus, she explained, he did want to offer them jobs. He also wanted to provide the campers with food, medical care, and even concerts by the navy band.

The Bonus Marchers were delighted by the First Lady's visit. Afterward, one told a reporter, "Hoover sent the army. Roosevelt sent his wife!"[1]

When Franklin Roosevelt was sworn into office as the 32nd President of the United States, Eleanor said to a reporter: "There isn't going to be any First Lady. There is just going to be plain, ordinary Mrs. Roosevelt. And that is all."[2]

In a sense, she was right. Rather than serving primarily as the White House hostess, as other First Ladies had done, Eleanor preferred to be herself—busy serving others.

As First Lady, Eleanor traveled so much she earned

Throughout their long marriage, Eleanor steadfastly remained by her husband's side. Here she is seen holding him steady as he stands in his leg braces. With Eleanor's help, the polio-stricken President eventually learned to walk again.

the nickname "Eleanor Everywhere." In the first year alone, she traveled some 40,000 miles, crisscrossing the country to meet people, to give speeches, and to see firsthand the effects of the Great Depression. Since 1929 when the stock market crashed, thousands of people had been out of work, and homelessness and hunger were widespread.

Eleanor again served as her husband's eyes and ears as Franklin and his administration determined how best to help the American people. As Eleanor visited with coal miners, sharecroppers, factory workers, and other ordinary citizens from coast to coast, people began to feel that someone high up in government truly cared about their problems.

Franklin Roosevelt implemented a series of programs, known together as the New Deal, to help America prosper again. Eleanor became involved in a number of these programs, including the National Youth Administration and the Works Progress Administration.

As part of the New Deal's intent to help create financial security for all Americans, Franklin signs the Social Security Act in 1935.

My Day · By Eleanor Roosevelt

WASHINGTON, Tuesday.—Yesterday, in New York City, was a busy day spent almost entirely on personal things. I had an interesting talk with a young Korean woman, married to an American citizen, who has been promoting an organization among the women of her community which she thinks would be of value in many other communities.

Her hope was that I would head up this organization on a nation-wide basis, but I feel very strongly that everything that is done should originate in a community need and, therefore, should enlist the interest and activity of the people in a particular community. National plans smack too much of something handed down from the top. Though I think it is well when something valuable is done in any community to have it given wide publicity so that other communities with the same needs may adopt it, I think it is a mistake to try to start any new national organizations at this time.

* * *

I was interested in an appeal which I received the other day. It was from one of the community organizations in my home state. They explained that they felt benefits and large mass meetings should be the methods used to raise money for the extraordinary war activities. That the usual community organizations, both charitable and civic, should obtain their support simply by reminding their subscribers of the need in the community. I think this theory is excellent and hope that we shall prove good enough citizens to put it into practice successfully.

I meant to find time to go to see an exhibition of paintings at the Grand Central Fifth Avenue Galleries in the Hotel Gotham yesterday, while in New York City. These are paintings of New England by Robert Strong Woodward. Since I know so much of the countryside he paints, I looked forward with great pleasure to seeing them. Unfortunately, I did not get there and the exhibition closes on the 14th of March, and I cannot be in New York City again until the 15th. This is a real disappointment and I hope he will hold another exhibition somewhere else before long.

* * *

We came back to Washington this morning by train in order to do as much work as possible on the way, and now I am about to keep a few appointments here.

Eleanor Roosevelt loved to read and was a prolific writer. Her famous *My Day* newspaper column ran for twenty-seven years. She also penned her autobiography and authored or coauthored thirteen more books on such issues as politics, travel, parenting, and world peace. She wrote two books for children: *A Trip to Washington with Bobby and Betty* and *Christmas: A Story*.

As First Lady, Eleanor also met and entertained many celebrities and world leaders—prime ministers, military leaders, kings and queens—but her heart was always with the common people. When she was invited to write a column for *Women's Home Companion*, her first article was titled, "I Want You to Write to Me." Eleanor wanted people to tell her about their lives and their problems so that she and Franklin could help to solve them. Over the next year, she received 300,000 letters!

Franklin and Eleanor's goal was for a government that directly helped the American people. The Great Depression spanned the entire decade of the 1930s, and the Roosevelts worked tirelessly to turn the tide on joblessness and poverty. This vision of government became known in Washington as the Roosevelt Way.

By 1940, the country began to ease its way back to a more stable economy, but soon the Roosevelt administration was to face its second great challenge. On December 7, 1941, the Japanese Army attacked American forces at Pearl Harbor in Hawaii, and the United States entered World War II. Franklin and Eleanor were not exempt from the heartaches of war; all four of their sons were drafted into service and sent overseas. Thankfully, all four survived.

Throughout the war years, "Eleanor Everywhere" continued her travels. When Franklin asked her to be a goodwill ambassador for the troops overseas, she happily agreed. She flew thousands of miles to visit troops in Europe, Latin America, and the South Pacific. Soldiers were surprised and gladdened when Eleanor suddenly appeared in barracks, on ships, in hospitals, and at Red Cross canteens. Everywhere she went, she encouraged the soldiers, telling them they were doing a wonderful job and they were

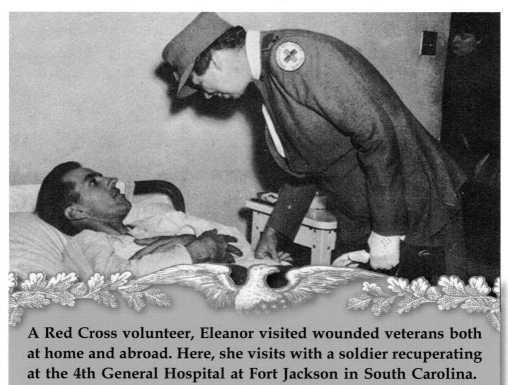

A Red Cross volunteer, Eleanor visited wounded veterans both at home and abroad. Here, she visits with a soldier recuperating at the 4th General Hospital at Fort Jackson in South Carolina.

Eleanor Roosevelt with members of the Tuskegee Airmen

not forgotten back home. *The New York Times* quoted one wounded soldier as saying, "Over here, she was something . . . none of us had seen in over a year, an American mother."[3]

As First Lady, Eleanor was well known for defying tradition, becoming the first president's wife to do many things. For instance, to show her support of the U.S. Army's Tuskegee Airmen, the first all–African American military aviation unit, she flew for an hour with pilot and instructor C. Alfred "Chief" Anderson. Later named the Fighter Squadron, the Tuskegee Airmen became the first squadron of black pilots to fight in World War II. Eleanor was also the first to hold her own press conferences (with, at her insistence, only female reporters in attendance). She was the first wife of a president to speak at a national political convention. She was the first to insist on driving her own car, and the first to routinely fly around the country. She was also the first to host a weekly radio show.

Eleanor was also the first—and last—wife of a president to serve four terms in the White House. Eleanor Roosevelt was First Lady for a total of twelve years, one month, one week, and one day.[4]

Eleanor Roosevelt becomes the first First Lady to hold a press conference.

Equal Rights for All

At a time when segregation was widely accepted, Eleanor Roosevelt worked to gain equal rights for America's black citizens. Years before her highly publicized flight with Tuskegee pilot Chief Anderson, she became the first president's wife to allow herself to be photographed with African Americans.

In 1934, Eleanor began to work closely with Walter White, the director of the National Association for the Advancement of Colored People (NAACP). She joined the local chapter of the NAACP, becoming the first white resident of Washington, D.C., to do so. She eventually became a board member.

When the Southern Conference for Human Welfare met in Birmingham, Alabama, in 1938, Eleanor attended. She entered the auditorium intending to sit with her good friend, black educator Mary McLeod Bethune. Once she sat down, however, police told her she was breaking the law by sitting on the black side of the auditorium. She was asked to move to the white side. Eleanor refused. Not wanting to break the law, however, she placed a chair in the center aisle and sat directly between the white side and the black side.

The following year, the Daughters of the American Revolution (DAR) refused to allow a famous black opera singer, Marian Anderson, to give a concert at Constitution Hall. Though Eleanor was proud of her ancestors who had taken part in the Revolutionary War, she decided she could no longer belong to an organization that practiced racism. She promptly and publicly resigned from the DAR.

Many people criticized Eleanor for her outspokenness on civil rights, but she never quit fighting for equal rights for all.

Chapter Five
ON HER OWN

Franklin Roosevelt died suddenly of a stroke on April 12, 1945, just as the war was drawing to a close. He had been vacationing in Warm Springs, Georgia, and Eleanor wasn't with him. She was speaking at a fund-raiser in Washington when she received the call.

She returned to the White House and summoned Vice President Harry S Truman. When he arrived, she told him the president was dead. He was stunned, and asked if there was anything he could do for her.

Eleanor famously responded, "Is there anything *we* can do for *you*? For you are the one in trouble now."

Franklin was buried in the rose garden of the family home at Hyde Park. After forty years of marriage, Eleanor was on her own. But President Truman wasn't about to let Eleanor be idle. He knew that with her vast knowledge and experience, she could continue to be a valuable asset to America, and he had plenty of work for her to do.

At the end of World War II, newly peaceful countries formed the United Nations, an international organization created to work for peace and political stability around the world. Only months after Franklin's death,

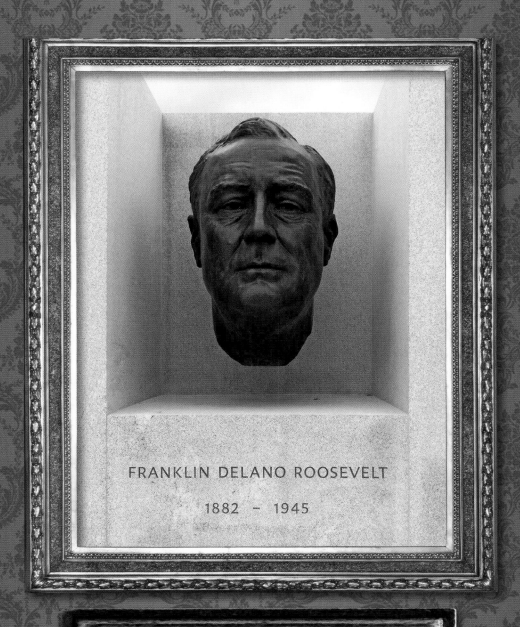

FRANKLIN DELANO ROOSEVELT

1882 – 1945

A bust of the former president greets visitors to the Franklin D. Roosevelt Four Freedoms Park on Roosevelt Island in New York City.

Eleanor Roosevelt speaks at the United Nations.

Truman appointed Eleanor as a delegate to the first meeting of the United Nations General Assembly. She was one of only five U.S. delegates chosen, and the only woman.

The following year, 1946, Eleanor was elected chairperson of the UN Commission on Human Rights. The commission was given the task of drafting a Universal Declaration of Human Rights. Eleanor and the other members worked hard on the declaration for two years and eight months. Finally, on December 10, 1948, Eleanor presented the declaration to the UN General Assembly. The Assembly voted to adopt it by a vote of 48-0. Following this important accomplishment, the Assembly gave Eleanor a standing ovation. The declaration has been translated into the native languages of all countries and remains the principal guide to assessing a country's treatment of its people.

Eleanor served at the UN through the Truman administration, but when Dwight D. Eisenhower took office as president, she resigned. Afterward, she stayed busy writing articles, hosting her radio broadcasts, working with the Girl Scouts of America, and supporting civil rights. In 1959 she began hosting a monthly television program, *Prospects of Mankind*, and in 1960 she actively campaigned for Democrat John F. Kennedy for president.

In her personal life, she divided her time between her New York apartment and her cottage named Val-Kill at Hyde Park. She cherished time spent with her many friends and her children, grandchildren, and great-grandchildren. For a former First Lady, she was very down-to-earth in her daily habits. She continued to drive herself everywhere she went, did her own shopping at roadside stands, and wore cotton dresses and comfortable tennis shoes to church on Sundays. In her few quiet hours she enjoyed reading, knitting, working in her garden, and walking her Scottish terrier, Fala. The former First Dog remained Eleanor's beloved companion until his death in 1952.

After John F. Kennedy was elected President, he reappointed Eleanor to the United Nations in 1961 and named her to the Advisory

Eleanor and Fala

Council of the Peace Corps. He also appointed Eleanor as head of the newly formed President's Commission on the Status of Women. As always, she took her responsibilities seriously and worked hard for the causes in which she believed.

Even into her late sixties and seventies, she continued to be "Eleanor Everywhere," traveling both on behalf of the United States and as a private citizen. Her travels took her to Japan, Israel, India, Morocco, and the Soviet Union. She spoke not just with world leaders but also, through interpreters, with the common people. She wanted to learn about their culture and how they lived. She wanted to know what their problems were and how their lives could be improved. She often said, "About the only value my life may have is to show that one can, even without any particular gifts, overcome obstacles that seem insurmountable if one is willing to face the fact that they must be overcome; that, in spite of timidity and fear, in spite of a lack of special talents, one can find a way to live widely and fully."

The "plain, ordinary Mrs. Roosevelt" lived a truly remarkable life of tireless service to others. Her example is an inspiration, no matter a person's talents or abilities, to find a way to live widely and fully and to make a difference in the world.

By the summer of 1962, she could no longer shake off increasing feelings of weakness and pain. She was hospitalized and diagnosed with a blood disease called aplastic anemia. She returned to her apartment where friends, family, and around-the-clock nurses cared for her. On November 7, 1962, Eleanor Roosevelt died at the age of 78.[1]

At the news of Eleanor's death, flags flew at half-mast all across the United States. It was the first time this honor had been given to a woman. President John F. Kennedy called her one of the great ladies in the history of our country, while former President Truman remarked that Eleanor Roosevelt was the First Lady of the World.

Knowing Eleanor as we do now, we can imagine she was most pleased by the comments made by ordinary Americans, such as this from a Bronx truck driver: "The folks will miss her. She was always on their side."[2]

Eleanor's Legacy

Upon her death in 1962, *The New York Times* hailed Eleanor Roosevelt as "one of the most esteemed women in the world."[3] Throughout her lifetime, honors and awards were showered upon her in recognition of her work. She received 35 honorary degrees from universities around the world, including Smith College (United States), Oxford University (England), and University of Lyon (France). She also received dozens of awards for her humanitarian efforts from such diverse organizations as the National Education Association of America, the Women's Zionist Organization of America, the National Council of Negro Women, and the National Society for Crippled Children and Adults (Easter Seals). Three times she was nominated for the Nobel Peace Prize, and though she didn't win, she was posthumously awarded the United Nations Human Rights Prize in 1968. Also after her death, in 1973, she was inducted into the National Women's Hall of Fame for her efforts on behalf of minorities.

Today, the name Eleanor Roosevelt graces numerous awards given to men and women who, like Eleanor, have devoted themselves to humanitarian causes. One of these is the Eleanor Roosevelt Val-Kill Medal Awards. It is given to up to a half dozen recipients each year for their contributions to society through the arts, education, philanthropy, and community service.

Another award that bears Eleanor's name is The Eleanor Roosevelt Award for Human Rights. Established in 1998 by U.S. Secretary of State Madeleine Albright, it is bestowed annually upon four recipients for their outstanding work in promoting and protecting human rights both in the United States and abroad.

Eleanor Roosevelt statue

1884   Anna Eleanor Roosevelt is born on October 11 in New York City to Elliott and Anna Roosevelt.

1892   Eleanor is placed in the care of her grandmother, Mary Hall, after the death of her mother. Her father dies in 1894.

1899   Eleanor enrolls as a student at Allenswood School in England.

1903   After returning to New York to make her social debut, Eleanor begins teaching at the Rivington Street Settlement House.

1905   Eleanor and Franklin Delano Roosevelt marry on March 17.

1906   The first of their six children is born. One child dies in infancy.

1917   The United States enters World War I. Franklin is assistant secretary of the navy. Eleanor begins volunteer work.

1921   Franklin is stricken with polio. Eleanor becomes her husband's eyes and ears as she immerses herself in Democratic Party politics.

1928   Upon her husband's election as governor, Eleanor becomes First Lady of New York.

1932   When Franklin takes office as U.S. President, Eleanor becomes First Lady of the United States.

1933–1945 During Franklin's four terms in the White House, Eleanor tirelessly crusades for the rights of minorities, including women, African Americans, child laborers, and war refugees.

1941 Eleanor shows her support of the Tuskegee Airmen in March. The United States enters World War II in December. Throughout the war, Eleanor travels to Europe, Latin America, and the South Pacific as a goodwill ambassador to American troops.

1945 Franklin dies during his fourth term in office. World War II ends. President Harry S Truman appoints Eleanor as a U.S. delegate to the United Nations.

1946 Eleanor chairs the Human Rights Commission of the United Nations, which creates the Universal Declaration of Human Rights. She resigns her post in 1953.

1961 President John F. Kennedy reappoints Eleanor as a UN delegate and head of the Commission on the Status of Women.

1962 Eleanor dies on November 7 at the age of 78.

1968 Eleanor is posthumously awarded the United Nations Human Rights Prize.

1973 Eleanor is inducted into the National Women's Hall of Fame.

1998 The Eleanor Roosevelt Award for Human Rights is established.

Chapter 1. Little Nell

1. Eleanor Roosevelt, *The Autobiography of Eleanor Roosevelt* (New York: Harper & Brothers, 1961), p. 12.

2. Geoffrey C. Ward and Ken Burns, *The Roosevelts: An Intimate History* (New York: Alfred A. Knopf, 2014), p. 3.

3. Blanche Wiesen Cook, *Eleanor Roosevelt, Volume 1* (New York: Penguin Books, 1992), p. 167.

Chapter 2. Dancing to a Different Drummer

1. Eleanor Roosevelt, *The Autobiography of Eleanor Roosevelt* (New York: Harper & Brothers, 1961), p. 37.

2. Geoffrey C. Ward and Ken Burns, *The Roosevelts: An Intimate History* (New York: Alfred A. Knopf, 2014), p. 116.

3. Roosevelt, p. 41.

4. Ibid., p. 63.

5. Ibid., p. 61.

6. Ibid., p. 113.

Chapter 3. Finding Her Place in Politics

1. Richard Harrity and Ralph C. Martin, *Eleanor Roosevelt: Her Life in Pictures* (New York: Duell, Sloan, and Pearce, 1958), pp. 89–90.

2. "First Lady Biography: Eleanor Roosevelt," *National First Ladies' Libraries,* accessed on November 7, 2014, http://www.firstladies.org/biographies/firstladies.aspx?biography=33

Chapter 4. A First for First Ladies

1. Geoffrey C. Ward and Ken Burns, *The Roosevelts: An Intimate History* (New York: Alfred A. Knopf, 2014), p. 307.

2. Lorena A. Hickok, *Reluctant First Lady: An Intimate Story of Eleanor Roosevelt's Early Public Life* (New York: Dodd, Mead & Co, 1962), http://archive.org/stream/reluctantfirstla012830mbp/reluctantfirstla012830mbp_djvu.txt

3. *The New York Times,* September 6, 1943, from *The Roosevelts: An Intimate History,* "The Common Cause," 2014, http://www.springfieldspringfield.co.uk/view_episode_scripts.php?tv-show=the-roosevelts-an-intimate-history-2014&episode=s01e06

4. "First Lady Biography: Eleanor Roosevelt," *National First Ladies' Libraries,* accessed on November 7, 2014, http://www.firstladies.org/biographies/firstladies.aspx?biography=33

Chapter 5. On Her Own

1. Geoffrey C. Ward and Ken Burns, *The Roosevelts: An Intimate History* (New York: Alfred A. Knopf, 2014), p. 473.

2. Robin McKown, *Eleanor Roosevelt's World* (New York: Grosset and Dunlap, 1964), p. 93.

3. "Mrs. Roosevelt, First Lady 12 Years, Often Called 'World's Most Admired Woman,' " *The New York Times,* November 8, 1962, via *On This Day,* accessed on January 6, 2015, http://www.nytimes.com/learning/general/onthisday/bday/1011.html

Books

Fleming, Candace. *Our Eleanor: A Scrapbook Look at Eleanor Roosevelt's Remarkable Life*. New York: Atheneum Books for Young Readers, 2005.

Hollingsworth, Tamara. *Eleanor Roosevelt: A Friend to All* (Primary Source Readers: American Biographies). Huntington Beach, CA: Teacher Created Materials Publishing, 2010.

Rosenberg, Pam and Robin Gerber. *Eleanor Roosevelt: First Lady, Humanitarian, and World Citizen* (Spirit of America, Our People). North Mankato, MN: The Child's World Publishing, 2003; 2014 (Kindle).

Stille, Darlene R., *Eleanor Roosevelt: First Lady and Civil Rights Activist* (Beginner Biographies). Edina, MN: Magic Wagon, a division of ABDO Publishing, 2013.

Works Consulted

Cook, Blanche Wiesen. *Eleanor Roosevelt, Volume 1*. New York: Penguin Books, 1992.

Cook, Blanche Wiesen. *Eleanor Roosevelt, Volume 2*. New York: Penguin Books, 1999.

Harrity, Richard and Ralph C. Martin. *Eleanor Roosevelt: Her Life in Pictures*. New York: Duell, Sloan, and Pearce, 1958.

Hickok, Lorena A. *Reluctant First Lady: An Intimate Story of Eleanor Roosevelt's Early Public Life*. New York: Dodd, Mead & Co, 1962.

McKown, Robin. *Eleanor Roosevelt's World*. New York: Grosset and Dunlap, 1964.

Roosevelt, Eleanor. *The Autobiography of Eleanor Roosevelt*. New York: Harper & Brothers, 1961.

Ward, Geoffrey C., and Ken Burns. *The Roosevelts: An Intimate History*. New York: Alfred A. Knopf, 2014.

On the Internet

The Eleanor Roosevelt Papers Project. "Eleanor Roosevelt and Civil Rights." http://www.gwu.edu/~erpapers/teachinger/lesson-plans/notes-er-and-civil-rights.cfm

Franklin D. Roosevelt Presidential Library and Museum: Biography of Eleanor Roosevelt
http://www.fdrlibrary.marist.edu/education/resources/bio_er.html

Live the History: Eleanor Roosevelt
http://www.historynet.com/eleanor-roosevelt

National First Ladies' Libraries: Eleanor Roosevelt
http://www.firstladies.org/biographies/firstladies.aspx?biography=33

The White House: Anna Eleanor Roosevelt
http://www.whitehouse.gov/about/first-ladies/eleanorroosevelt

administration (ad-mih-nih-STRAY-shun)—The government officials who work under a president.

alderman (AHL-der-mun)—A person on the governing council of a city or town.

ambassador (am-BAS-uh-dur)—Someone who travels from one group of people to another to forge friendships and promote ideals.

belle (BEL)—A pretty young woman.

calisthenics (kal-is-THEH-niks)—Exercises done without weights or other equipment, such as sit-ups and push-ups.

campaign (kam-PAYN)—A series of speeches, meetings, advertisements, and other actions done in order to win votes.

candidate (KAN-dih-dayt)—A person seeking political office.

debutant (DEB-yoo-tahnt)—A young woman being introduced into society for the first time.

delegate (DEL-ih-git)—A person who represents and speaks for others.

descendant (dih-SEN-dunt)—A person's child or later offspring.

diphtheria (dip-THEER-ee-uh)—A serious contagious disease in which the throat becomes blocked, marked by fever and difficulty breathing.

eligible (EL-ih-juh-bul)—Suitable for marriage.

encampment (en-CAMP-ment)—A campsite or place of temporary dwelling.

exempt (ek-ZEMPT)—Not subject to a rule or obligation.

grievance (GREE-vunts)—Complaint.

immigrant (IH-muh-grunt)—One who moves into a new country.

invalid (IN-vuh-lid)—One who is weak, sick, or disabled; unable to take care of oneself.

legislative (LEH-jih-slay-tiv)—From the branch of government that makes laws.

leisure (LEE-zur)—Not working for a living, but free and unoccupied.

nominate (NAH-mih-nayt)—To choose as a candidate for office.

pandemonium (pan-deh-MOH-nee-um)—Disorder; noise and confusion.

paralysis (puh-RAL-uh-sis)—The inability to move parts of the body, such as the legs.

Parisian (pah-REE-zhen)—Of or from the city of Paris, France.

polio (POH-lee-oh)—Short for poliomyelitis (poh-lee-oh-my-uh-LY-tis), a disease that can cause paralysis.

pompadour (POM-puh-dor)—A hairstyle in which the hair is swept up from the face and worn high over the forehead, and sometimes also swept up around the sides and back.

prolific (proh-LIH-fik)—Producing much of something.

prominent (PRAH-muh-nent)—Well-known; standing out.

safeguard—To protect.

segregation (seh-grah-GAY-shun)—The practice of keeping people of different races apart.

tenement (TEH-nuh-munt) **house**—A large building divided into apartments that are usually run-down and overcrowded.

Ann Tatlock is a novelist and children's book author. Her works have received numerous awards, including the Silver Angel Award from Excellence in Media and the Midwest Book Award. She lives in the Blue Ridge Mountains of Western North Carolina with her husband and daughter.